THIRD GRADE GEOGRAPHY:
EARTHQUAKES AND VOLCANOES

SPEEDY
PUBLISHING

Speedy Publishing LLC
40 E. Main St. #1156
Newark, DE 19711
www.speedypublishing.com

Copyright 2015

Volcanic eruptions are usually preceded by earthquakes large and small.

EARTHQUAKES

Earthquakes are the shaking, rolling or sudden shock of the earth's surface. They are the Earth's natural means of releasing stress.

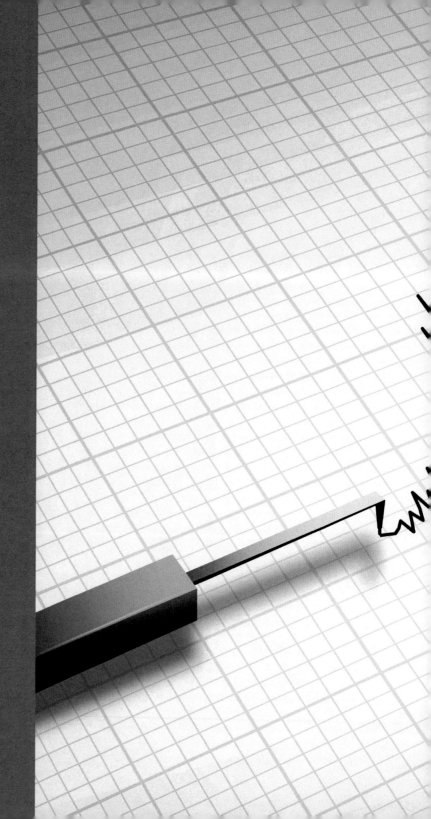

A seismograph
is an instrument
used for recording
the intensity and
duration of an
earthquake.

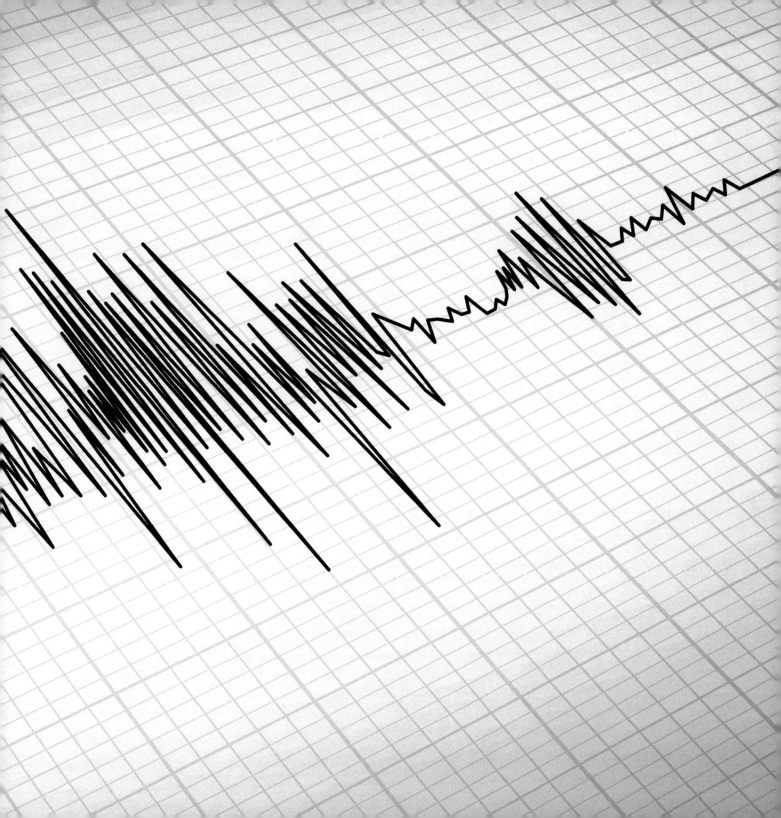

Underneath the Earth's surface lie tectonic plates. When the plates squeeze or stretch, huge rocks form at their edges and the rocks shift with great force, causing an earthquake.

VOLCANOES

Volcanoes are openings in the Earth's surface. When they are active they spew lava, rock, poisonous gases and ash with great power.

The word volcano
originally comes
from the name of
the Roman god
of fire, Vulcan.

Hot liquid rock under the Earth's surface is known as magma, it is called lava after it comes out of a volcano.